OCEANS ALIVE

Lionfish

by Colleen Sexton

BELLWETHER MEDIA · MINNEAPOLIS BADGER PUBLIC LIBRARY

Note to Librarians, Teachers, and Parents:

Blastoff! Readers are carefully developed by literacy experts and combine standards-based content with developmentally appropriate text.

Level 1 provides the most support through repetition of high-frequency words, light text, predictable sentence patterns, and strong visual support.

Level 2 offers early readers a bit more challenge through varied simple sentences, increased text load, and less repetition of high-frequency words.

Level 3 advances early-fluent readers toward fluency through increased text and concept load, less reliance on visuals, longer sentences, and more literary language.

Level 4 builds reading stamina by providing more text per page, increased use of punctuation, greater variation in sentence patterns, and increasingly challenging vocabulary.

Level 5 encourages children to move from "learning to read" to "reading to learn" by providing even more text, varied writing styles, and less familiar topics.

Whichever book is right for your reader, Blastoff! Readers are the perfect books to build confidence and encourage a love of reading that will last a lifetime!

This edition first published in 2009 by Bellwether Media, Inc.

No part of this publication may be reproduced in whole or in part without written permission of the publisher. For information regarding permission, write to Bellwether Media, Inc., Attention: Permissions Department, Post Office Box 19349, Minneapolis, MN 55419.

Library of Congress Cataloging-in-Publication Data
Sexton, Colleen A., 1967–
   Lionfish / by Colleen Sexton.
      p. cm. – (Blastoff! readers. Oceans alive)
   Includes bibliographical references and index.
   Summary: "Simple text and supportive images introduce beginning readers to lionfish. Intended for students in kindergarten through third grade"–Provided by publisher.
   ISBN-13: 978-1-60014-250-5 (hardcover : alk. paper)
   ISBN-10: 1-60014-250-8 (hardcover : alk. paper)
   1. Pterois volitans–Juvenile literature. I. Title.

   QL638.S42S49 2009
   597'.68–dc22   2008033541

Contents

Lionfish live near **coral reefs** in warm, shallow waters.

Lionfish are hunters.
They move along the reef
at night to search for **prey**.

Lionfish rest during the day.
They hide in cracks in the reef.

Lionfish have a rounded body that ends in a tail.

Lionfish have stripes. The stripes can be red, yellow, white, or black.

8

gills

Lionfish breathe through **gills**.

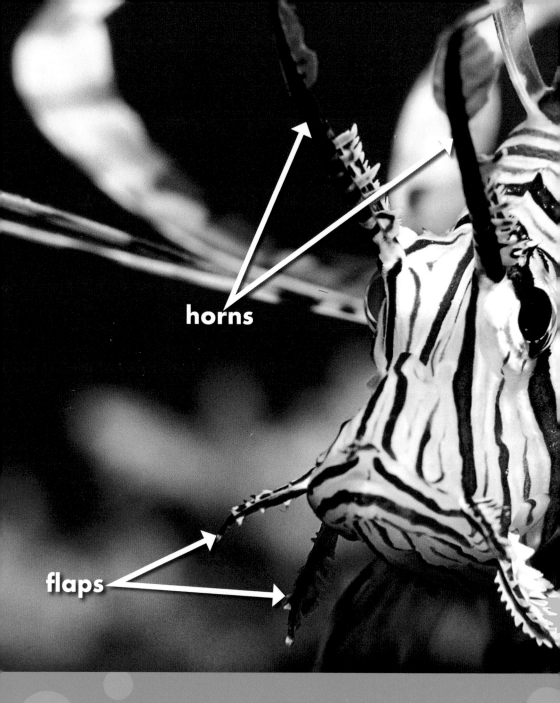

horns

flaps

Lionfish have thick flaps
of skin above and below
their mouths.

Lionfish have two horns that stick out above their eyes.

Lionfish have long **fins**.
Some fins look like feathers.
Others are clear with stripes.

Lionfish fan out their fins to hunt. They can use their fins to trap prey in small spaces.

Some lionfish stay still and wait for fish, shrimp, and crabs to come by.

The lionfish open their mouths and suck in their prey whole.

Lionfish have long, sharp **spines** between their fins.

spines

Lionfish can use their spines to sting. Poison comes out of the tips of some spines.

17

A lionfish uses its spines to protect itself and its **territory**.

The lionfish gets ready to attack if another hunter swims into its territory.

The lionfish spreads its fins
and raises its spines.

Whoosh! The other hunter swims away before the lionfish attacks.

Glossary

coral reef—a structure in the ocean made of the skeletons of many small, tube-shaped animals called corals

fins—flaps on a fish's body used for moving, steering, and stopping in the water

gills—organs near the mouth that a fish uses to breathe; the gills move oxygen from the water to the fish's blood.

prey—an animal that is hunted by another animal for food

spine—a hard, sharp part on an animal or plant; the lionfish's spines are poisonous.

territory—an area that animals live in and defend

To Learn More

AT THE LIBRARY

Lundblad, Kristina and Bobbie Kalman. *Animals Called Fish.* New York: Crabtree, 2005.

Pfeffer, Wendy. *What's It Like to Be a Fish?* New York: HarperCollins, 1996.

Sill, Cathryn P. *About Fish: A Guide for Children.* Atlanta, Ga.: Peachtree, 2002.

ON THE WEB

Learning more about lionfish is as easy as 1, 2, 3.

1. Go to www.factsurfer.com.

2. Enter "lionfish" into the search box.

3. Click the "Surf" button and you will see a list of related Web sites.

With factsurfer.com, finding more information is just a click away.

Index